Saint Elizabeth Ann Seton

Saint Elizabeth Ann Seton

Daughter of America

Written by
Jeanne Marie Grunwell

Illustrated by
Mari Goering

BOOKS & MEDIA

Boston

Library of Congress Cataloging-in-Publication Data

Grunwell, Jeanne Marie.
   Saint Elizabeth Ann Seton : daughter of
America / written by Jeanne Marie Grunwell ;
illustrated by Mari Goering.
     p. cm. — (Encounter the saints series ; 3)
   Summary: Biography of the woman who was a
wife, mother, widow, foundress and member of a
religious congregation, and convert to the Catholic
faith as well as the first American-born saint.
   ISBN 0-8198-7022-6 (pbk.)
   1. Seton, Elizabeth Ann, Saint, 1774–1821—
Juvenile literature.   2. Christian saints—United
States—Biography.   [1. Seton, Elizabeth Ann,   Saint,
1774–1821. 2. Saints. 3. Women— Biography.] I.
Goering, Mari, 1948– ill.
   II. Title.   III. Series.
   BX4700.S4G78   1999
   271'.9102—dc21
   [B]   99-18672
                                     CIP

Printed and published in the U.S.A. by Pauline Books &
Media, 50 Saint Pauls Avenue, Boston, MA 02130-3491.
www.pauline.org
Pauline Books & Media is the publishing house of the
Daughters of St. Paul, an international congregation of
women religious serving the Church with the communi-
cations media.

3 4 5 6 7 8   07 06 05 04 03 02

Encounter the Saints Series

Blesseds Jacinta and
Francisco Marto
Shepherds of Fatima

Journeys with Mary
Apparitions of Our Lady

Saint Anthony
of Padua
Fire and Light

Saint Bernadette
Soubirous
Light in the Grotto

Saint Edith Stein
Blessed by the Cross

Saint Elizabeth
Ann Seton
Daughter of America

Saint Francis
of Assisi
Gentle Revolutionary

Saint Ignatius
of Loyola
*For the Greater
Glory of God*

Saint Isaac Jogues
With Burning Heart

Saint Joan of Arc
God's Soldier

Saint Juan Diego
*And Our Lady of
Guadalupe*

Saint Julie Billiart
The Smiling Saint

Saint Maximilian
Kolbe
Mary's Knight

Saint Pio
of Pietrelcina
Rich in Love

For other children's titles on the Saints,
visit our Web site: www.pauline.org

CONTENTS

1

CHANGES

The year was 1774. New York was still one of the thirteen British colonies and the United States didn't exist yet. But New York was already one of the busiest cities in the New World. It had banks and churches, colleges and stores, and a harbor that could hold three hundred white-sailed cutty ships all at once.

New York could also boast of its hospitals and doctors. One of the city's finest young physicians was Dr. Richard Bayley. His wife, Catherine Charlton, was the daughter of an Episcopalian minister. The couple had a little daughter named Mary.

On August 28, 1774, a second daughter was born to the Bayleys. Dr. and Mrs. Bayley named their new infant Elizabeth Ann. She was soon baptized at Holy Trinity Episcopal Church.

One week after Elizabeth was born, the first Continental Congress met in Philadelphia. The thirteen American colonies wanted to declare their independence from Great

Britain. Before long, the colonies were at war. Men had to choose sides. They argued.

"I say we should side with the motherland. Who knows how this foolish revolution will end?"

"You're right. Besides, belonging to England gives us security."

"Foolishness! Security! To desire freedom is not foolish, gentlemen. As for security, all we can count on from Great Britain are more taxes! We need our independence!"

It was a confusing time.

When the American Revolution began, Dr. Bayley was away in England studying medicine. He had many friends there. He arrived back home in New York on July 12, 1776—dressed in a British army uniform.

"Richard!" his wife gasped as she opened the front door.

"Hush! Don't be frightened, Catherine," Dr. Bayley soothed. "Everything is all right. I've joined the British army as a surgeon."

A few short weeks later, Dr. Bayley was off again, this time traveling with the British fleet. He spent many months away from his family. During those months British troops occupied New York. In an attempt to stop their advance, some patriots set fire one night to a small house on one of the wharves.

Within minutes the blaze exploded out of control. It swept through the city, destroying everything in its path. Trinity Church was burned to the ground and Elizabeth Ann Bayley's baptismal records were destroyed.

Elizabeth was too young to remember much about the war raging around her. But then something happened that would change her life—forever.

In the chill of the early morning, Elizabeth awoke to hushed sounds coming from her mother's bedroom. Mrs. Bayley had just given birth to a baby girl. But now the young mother was dying. Dr. Bayley arrived in time to have her die in his arms. He tearfully named the new baby Catherine, after his wife.

"Mommy, Mommy!" two-year-old Elizabeth whimpered as strangers continued to bustle in and out of the bedroom. But no one seemed to pay any attention.

2

A NEW MOTHER

A year passed. Dr. Bayley felt his three little girls needed a mother to look after them. He met Amelia Charlotte Barclay, and soon they were married.

"Come now, give your new mother a kiss," Dr. Bayley coaxed. Mary and Elizabeth solemnly obeyed. Baby Catherine cooed. But somehow, things were different. An icy feeling separated the girls from their new mother. They never called Amelia "Mommy." Instead she was "Mrs. Bayley."

When Elizabeth was four, Catherine, or "Kit," as everyone called her, died. Elizabeth sat by herself on the doorstep while the grown-ups gathered inside for the funeral. She looked up at the clouds. "How beautiful it must be in heaven," she imagined. The thought made her smile. Just then her Uncle William slipped outside. He sat down beside Elizabeth.

"Betty, didn't you cry when your baby sister Kitty died?" he asked softly.

Elizabeth shook her head. "No, Uncle William."

"Why not?"

"Because Kitty is gone up to heaven. I wish I could go, too, and be with Mama and Kit."

Uncle William picked up little Elizabeth and placed her on his lap. He drew her head to his heart, stroking her curly hair. "Betty," he said quietly, "someday, we will all be happy together in heaven."

After that day Elizabeth often thought of her mother and little Kitty in heaven. One evening, just as the sun was setting, Elizabeth carried her new baby half-sister up the attic stairs. "Look, Emma! See how beautiful!" she whispered, pointing out the window to the setting sun. "See where God lives? He lives up in heaven. Someday we'll go to live with him too," she promised, "someday."

Elizabeth wanted more than anything to go to heaven, and she tried hard to be good. But it wasn't always easy. She had a fiery temper which showed itself in different ways. For one thing, she hated having to study French and music. "But why do I have to?" she'd demand with a stomp of her foot. "Why?"

Within eight years, Amelia and Dr. Bayley had six children. Mary and Elizabeth had trouble getting along with their new mother, and Amelia often paid less attention to them than to her own children. On top of it all, Dr. Bayley spent a lot of time away from home. His days were filled with making house calls or working at the hospital. He was up nights caring for the sick, especially the European immigrants who now flooded New York Harbor, carrying with them contagious diseases. Elizabeth and her older sister Mary felt more lonely than ever. Then one day their father called for them.

"I have some news for the two of you," he announced. "I'd like you to go and live with Uncle William in New Rochelle for a while. I think it will be a nice change."

The girls looked at each other in surprise. Spending time at their uncle's 250-acre farm on Long Island Sound would be fun!

In New Rochelle Mary and Elizabeth were warmly welcomed by their Uncle William and Aunt Sarah, and their four cousins, William Jr., Susanne, Joseph, and Richard. Living on a farm was a whole new experience for the two sisters. Elizabeth liked to spend time by herself and found quiet moments for walking along the shore of the Sound collecting shells. She learned to speak French fluently with her cousins and finally learned to play the piano, becoming quite good at it. Mary, instead, was satisfied with studying the basics of arithmetic, reading, writing and sewing.

One day Uncle William hurriedly rode in from town. "There's great news!" he cried. "The war has ended! We've won our independence! George Washington will soon be marching up Broadway in a victory parade."

Aunt Sarah ran to the porch and excitedly rang the farm bell, calling everyone in from the fields. Such good news had to be shared!

3
Riot!

By 1786 Elizabeth was back at her father's house in New York. Dr. Bayley had become a professor of medicine at what is now Columbia University in New York City. He was respected around the world for his research on diseases like yellow fever and croup. Sometimes, in order to learn more about possible cures, he and his students studied the bodies of deceased persons.

One day some young boys were playing in the street just outside the hospital. A thoughtless student of Dr. Bayley's decided to play a cruel joke on them. He took an arm and waved it out the window yelling, "Here's the arm of your mother that spanked you well more than once!"

But the children didn't realize it was a joke. They ran home very frightened. The mother of one of the boys in the group had recently died. This little boy burst into his house looking for his father.

"Papa...is it...true...the doctors...have Mama's arm...at the hospital?" he panted.

"What's that you're saying?" the father asked in surprise.

"A man...just waved...an arm...at us...out the hospital window.... He said...it was Mama's," the trembling boy sobbed.

The father was furious and told friends and neighbors what had happened. Soon an angry mob surrounded the hospital. The people intended to punish the doctors and medical students. Breaking down the hospital doors, the crowd surged through the halls, smashing everything in its path— glass, furniture and laboratory equipment. The doctors and students, afraid of being killed, hid.

The next day, riots spread through the streets of New York. The rioters were looking for the doctors' families. They wanted revenge and they were ready to die before they gave up. Some did die. Police were sent to try and break up the fighting. Elizabeth heard the shouting and scuffling in the street. She knew that the throng outside was hunting for her family. That night, the Bayleys huddled close together in the dark, quiet and frightened. "Our Father, who art in heaven..." Elizabeth prayed over and over again. "Deliver us from evil."

Morning came. Carefully Elizabeth

pulled back the curtain and looked out the window. The street was deserted and quiet. The thirteen-year-old sighed in relief as she let the curtain fall.

The riot was over, but New York wasn't ready to forget the incident. Dr. Bayley, who had done so much good and risked his life for so many people, continued to meet with angry words and threats.

"Amelia," he said pensively one night, "for the safety of our family and the hospital, I've decided to set sail for England. Perhaps time will heal this bitterness."

Amelia nodded sadly.

"As for Mary and Elizabeth, it's best that they go back to William's for now," Dr. Bayley added. "I'll tell them in the morning."

4

Young Outcast

"I love it at Uncle William's, Betty, but I'm really going to miss Wright," Mary confided as the two sisters packed their things. "We want to get married, you know," she added dreamily.

Elizabeth folded her favorite dress and laid it in her suitcase. "As for me, I'll miss Father the most," she said quietly.

During the year he spent in England, Dr. Bayley never sent one letter to his family. Elizabeth worried. *Maybe he's sick,* she thought, *or even dead. Or maybe he just doesn't love us anymore.*

Elizabeth had no one but Mary to talk to about her pain. She didn't want to bother Uncle William or Aunt Sarah. And how could her cousins understand? She hid her sufferings from them all until one day her heart felt as if it would break into a million pieces. Elizabeth ran alone into the fields and sobbed. Slowly a sense of peace came over her. She remembered she had a Father in heaven who loved her. She felt God wrap her heart in a warm embrace.

Elizabeth drew closer to God during that year in New Rochelle. She read the Bible everyday. She fell in love with the wonders of nature. The birds' songs, the cloudless sky, the damp sand beneath her feet, everything was a gift from her heavenly Father. Everything was a proof of his love.

When Dr. Bayley finally returned from London early in 1790, Mary and Elizabeth went back to New York. Mary was married a few months later to Dr. Wright Post. But sixteen-year-old Elizabeth suddenly found herself all alone. After a disagreement with Mrs. Bayley, the stepmother made it clear that Elizabeth was no longer welcome at the Bayley home.

For the next four years, Elizabeth moved from house to house, depending on the generosity of other family members and friends. Most of the time she stayed with Mary and her husband. Elizabeth and her father grew very close to each other during this time. Dr. Bayley felt bad about her situation, but there was very little he could do. They wrote to each other often, but they hardly ever met outside of social functions.

Elizabeth was now old enough to attend society parties and dances. She enjoyed dancing and was very good at it. Soon she began attracting attention.

"Isn't Elizabeth Bayley lovely?" whispered high society ladies.

"Those large dark eyes and brown curls are very becoming. She'll make a perfect bride for some lucky young man."

"Well, don't say I told you so, but a very good source has seen *the* William Magee Seton with Elizabeth several times."

"They say he buys her presents and takes her to expensive places to dine. I wouldn't be at all surprised to hear of their engagement...."

The rumors were true. William Magee Seton did think that Elizabeth Bayley was one of the most beautiful women he had ever seen, and the whole of New York buzzed about the possibility of their marriage. William was six years older than Elizabeth and the handsome son of a wealthy New York businessman. He was tall and fair. Elizabeth was dark and petite. They made a perfect couple.

William took Elizabeth to balls and plays, where they mingled with the bustling city's upper class. Like the other society women, Elizabeth wore beautiful gowns and exquisite furs.

William sent his "Eliza" bouquets of expensive flowers from the city's first florist. The two constantly exchanged notes, calling each other by their own special nicknames. Elizabeth loved dancing and the theater, but more than anything else, she loved her "Will."

After they had dated for a year, William approached Dr. Bayley and formally asked for Elizabeth's hand in marriage. Dr. Bayley gave his consent, and the couple were married on January 25, 1794, by the pastor of the Episcopalian church. Will was twenty-five and Elizabeth was nineteen. Elizabeth had never been so happy.

5

MRS. SETON

Will had spent the whole day bumping across narrow dirt roads on a rickety stagecoach. It was difficult to write, but he didn't give up. He was scribbling a note to Elizabeth. And tomorrow he would write another. How he missed her! How he wished that his business trip were over and that he were home again!

The coach stopped in Newark, and Will mailed his letter. Then he unbuckled the travel bag Elizabeth had packed for him. He was surprised to see her beautiful face smiling up at him. His young wife, knowing Will would miss her as much as she would miss him, had tucked a miniature portrait of herself among his things.

"Oh! Elizabeth!" Will chuckled to himself, "only you would think of something like this!"

For the rest of the trip, Will showed the portrait to everyone he met. He wrote to Elizabeth about every compliment she received.

Elizabeth could hardly believe her joy. That fall, she was twenty years old and expecting her first child. She and Will had just moved into a house on Wall Street. It all seemed like a dream come true.

The couple's new residence was in a wealthy neighborhood, not far from the home of the famous patriot Alexander Hamilton. Will and Elizabeth's home was filled with beautiful furnishings, but most of all it was filled with love. Snug in front of the fire at night, Elizabeth wrote letters until her fingers grew cold, while Will entertained her with his violin.

On May 3, 1795, Elizabeth was writing to another good friend, Julia Scott, when she began to have labor pains. She begged Will to go downstairs and finish the letter. He happily did, scrawling a note to apologize that Elizabeth couldn't complete the letter because she was "indisposed," and then reporting that he and Elizabeth were the proud parents of a dark-eyed, rosy-cheeked baby girl named Anna Maria.

Anna was joined by a brother when William was born in November, 1796.

On February 22, 1797, Will was one of four men to host a spectacular sixty-fifth birthday ball for President George Washing-

"Will, you look so tired. Is anything wrong?"

ton. Elizabeth charmed the guests with her warm smile, her glistening jewels and her swirling gown as she swept across the ballroom in her husband's arms. But behind the smile, Elizabeth hid a secret worry.

"Will," she whispered between twirls, "you look so tired. Is anything wrong?"

"It's nothing, darling," he smiled back. "Just the 'Seton cough.' Don't you fret. I'm fine."

6

STORMY DAYS

The Seton family had suffered for years from the lung disease called consumption, known today as tuberculosis. In those days tuberculosis was incurable. Will had inherited the family's weak lungs, and had shown symptoms of the illness for as long as Elizabeth had known him. But now the dreaded cough was getting worse. Elizabeth was very concerned.

"Please, God, keep Will safe and well," she prayed. "Please." Elizabeth knew what tuberculosis could do. She knew that there was a very good chance that Will might die while still young.

"Elizabeth, I think doing some charitable work might distract you from your own problems," her pastor advised her one day. Following his suggestion, Elizabeth helped found the *Widows' Society* in New York in 1797. The Society raised money for the poor widows of the city. When Elizabeth listened to the women's terrible problems, her own seemed to become quite small. She thanked

God every day for Will, for their two healthy children, and for the third baby she was expecting. But little did Elizabeth know that she would soon have *seven* more children to care for....

During the winter of 1798, Will's father fell down the front steps of their house. He died that June as a result of the accident. As the oldest son, Will had to provide for his seven younger half-brothers and sisters still living at home. He and Elizabeth knew that ten children would never fit comfortably in their cozy home on Wall Street. They would have to move into his father's house on Stone Street—after the baby was born.

In the meantime, Elizabeth took up all the secretarial work for Will's business, which involved overseas trading. She worried when shipments were late in reaching their port of destination, and often learned that the cargo ships had been lost at sea, or pirated. She worked hard for many months and was ill during most of her third pregnancy. Her body was very weak and tired when it came time for the birth of her third child.

"What's wrong?" Elizabeth whispered as she read the panic in her father's eyes. Dr. Bayley didn't answer. He quickly bent over the newborn grandson he had just delivered. The urgency of his movements told Elizabeth the baby wasn't breathing. In the heat of that July morning, her father desperately struggled to fill the tiny lungs with his own breath. Finally, the baby cried. Elizabeth and Dr. Bayley hugged each other, laughing and crying at the same time.

"Little Richard," Elizabeth whispered as she cradled the tiny infant in her arms, "named after your grandfather who saved your life."

But the crisis wasn't over yet. It would take some time for Elizabeth to regain her health and strength. Richard was a weak baby and was soon sick again. So was Anna. So was Will. The deadly plague of yellow fever was sweeping through New York. It was no longer safe to remain in the city. Eighteen members of Elizabeth's family crowded together in a tiny summer home, waiting for the illness to pass as the cool weather set in. It was the end of September before they could go home. And home now meant their new house on Stone Street.

Elizabeth and Will first returned to Wall Street to pack up their family's belongings. That night Elizabeth warmed herself before the fireplace where she and Will had spent so many happy nights together. She sat down at her piano and gently touched the keys, feeling the music echo in her heart. Suddenly she broke into sobs. "Will, we will never again be in this room. Our life will never be the same."

Will embraced her, gently tilting back her head so that their eyes met. "It's true, Eliza, it's true," he whispered. "But we still have each other and our children. That's enough, isn't it?"

Elizabeth nodded and smiled through her tears. Will was right. And God would be there to help them face whatever the future held. Yes, it was more than enough.

7

NEW CHALLENGES

The large Seton house had to be cleaned and painted and wallpapered. It would be fun getting things ready for the rest of the family. Elizabeth had always wanted a large family. She wanted "to be able to teach the children about God and keep their little faces sparkling clean," as she once wrote in her diary when she was young. Now, God had fulfilled her dreams. She accepted his gift with joy.

The older Seton children were sent to boarding school. But eighteen-year-old Rebecca remained home to help Elizabeth take care of the younger Seton girls, Harriet and Cecilia, as well as Elizabeth's own children. Elizabeth had decided to teach the girls at home. She and Rebecca gave lessons every day from ten until two.

At first, Elizabeth and Rebecca didn't get along very well. Elizabeth thought her sister-in-law was silly and irresponsible. Rebecca thought Elizabeth was harsh and cold. But as they spent more time with each other, the two young women soon realized that they were both wrong. Elizabeth and Rebecca grew to love and respect each other very much. In time, Elizabeth even began to call Rebecca her "soul's sister," and her "dearest friend." Rebecca never left Elizabeth's side and tried to learn from her good example.

Almost every Sunday, Elizabeth and Rebecca went to church together to hear their friend, the Reverend John Henry Hobart, preach. They didn't want to miss even one of his energetic sermons.

"I know you're already working with the *Widow's Society*," the Reverend Hobart remarked one day, "but have you ever considered spending a little time helping the poor and the sick? There are so many of them in our city."

Elizabeth and Rebecca eagerly accepted Hobart's invitation. In fact, they became so dedicated to assisting the poor and the sick that their friends began calling them "Protestant Sisters of Charity," after the Catholic sisters who did similar work in France. Not that Elizabeth and Rebecca's friends had ever met a sister. There were hardly any Catholics living in New York at that time. If people were curious to see what a nun looked like, they had to visit the wax museum on Greenwich Street!

Raising a family and doing charity work kept Elizabeth busy, but she still found time for many other things. For fun she went to the theater with her sister Mary, or read a book whenever she had a few free minutes. She wrote letters to her friends, especially to Julia Scott and Eliza Sadler. In the evening she sat with an open Bible, studying her favorite scriptures and psalms.

After the death of Will's father, the Seton family business began losing money. Even though she was expecting another baby, Elizabeth often stayed up most of the night doing secretarial work for Will. She could see for herself how poorly the company was doing, and she wanted to lighten Will's burdens.

"Come to bed, Elizabeth," Will would beg. "It's past midnight."

"Let me just finish this last letter," she would say. Then, blowing out the lamp, Elizabeth would take Will's arm and the couple would tiptoe to their room, trying not to wake the children.

By Christmas of 1800, Will was bankrupt. The sheriffs came to repossess his family's valuables. He even had to turn over the key to his business.

Will felt like a total failure. He had a wife and four children (the youngest, Catherine, was just an infant), as well as seven brothers and sisters who were depending on him. Elizabeth's heart ached to see her husband's unhappiness. It worried her to see him growing weaker and more sickly due to the strain and hard work.

The family moved into a smaller house on the Battery, a park at the tip of Manhattan. The children played in the grass and watched ships sail in and out of the harbor. At night there were concerts with violins and singers. The wealthy people who strolled through the park paid fifty cents for ice cream and cake, punch and wine. But such luxuries were no longer a part of the Setons' lives.

8

THE FEVER

Will and Elizabeth now worried every day about how to feed and clothe their growing family. During the summer of 1801, Elizabeth and the children went to visit her father on nearby Staten Island, while Will traveled to Baltimore. Rebecca stayed behind to take care of the house.

Elizabeth was anxious about Will, and it upset her to be away from the Reverend Hobart and Rebecca.

One night, Anna saw her looking out the window across the bay.

"What are you looking at, Mama?" she asked.

"I see our house on the Battery," Elizabeth said softly, "and I wait for the lights to flicker or the shutters to move. Then I know that dear Rebecca is there, and we pray together."

Dr. Bayley, who had separated from his second wife several years earlier, spent the summer as Health Officer, treating the immigrants who continued to flock to New York. They spilled out of crowded, filthy ships, kissing the ground as they stepped onto dry land for the first time in weeks. Starving and sick, the immigrants were packed together in tents and shacks. Many died there.

Elizabeth followed her father to the quarantined area one day. She was so saddened by the immigrants' suffering that she asked him if she could help, and nurse the babies on her mother's milk. "You shall do no such thing!" Dr. Bayley shouted, ordering Elizabeth to go home for fear she would catch the plague.

Dr. Bayley worked long hours each day. But he was never too tired to spend time with his grandchildren. He grinned as he held baby Catherine, whom everyone called "Kit," in his lap, coaxing her to say "Papa."

"Papa! Papa!" Kit would mimic.

Elizabeth wrote to her friends Eliza and Julia, asking for the music to Dr. Bayley's favorite songs. She played these for him on the piano. She was happy now that she had been forced to study music in school! After so many years of separation, these hours spent with her father were treasured times for Elizabeth.

Early one August morning, when the plague was at its worst, Dr. Bayley came home from the quarantine station feeling sick. After breakfast Elizabeth looked out the window. She saw her father sitting on a log in the hot sun, his face in his hands. Putting baby Kit down, she ran outside.

Dr. Bayley looked up in confusion. "I'm... not feeling well," he managed to mumble.

Elizabeth burst into tears. She realized that her father had finally contracted yellow fever. With the help of a servant, she managed to get him to bed. He immediately became delirious. For days Elizabeth sat by his side. Her sister Mary and brother-in-law Dr. Post came to help. Together they fought to bring Dr. Bayley through the plague. But nothing helped. "Thy will be done," Elizabeth prayed over and over. "Father, thy will be done."

At a certain point her father opened his eyes and recognized Elizabeth by his side.

"I know what's coming, Elizabeth," he whispered hoarsely. "All the horrors of this disease...I've seen them so many times. And now I feel them all. Cover me with a blanket, as I have covered so many poor little children."

The ravages of yellow fever lasted an entire week. The end finally came on August 17, 1801. Elizabeth held her father's hand as he peacefully took his last breath.

9

To Italy

"If only Father could be here to see you," Elizabeth murmured to the tiny baby she cuddled in her arms, "he'd be so proud of you."

It was August 19, 1802—just two days after the first anniversary of Dr. Bayley's death—and Elizabeth and Will were celebrating new life with baby Rebecca, their fifth child.

Soon after Bec was born, Will began going to church with Elizabeth. She could see Will drawing closer to God and this made her feel all the closer to him. Elizabeth could hardly imagine life without Will. But she couldn't help noticing that his health was growing worse and worse.

"Will, maybe a change of climate would help you. Why don't we sail to Italy?" Elizabeth proposed one day. "We could visit your friends, the Filicchis, at Leghorn. The mountain air and sun would do you good, I just know they would!" Elizabeth could see that she was convincing Will. She smiled and added. "We could even take Anna along. She'd love it!"

Will easily gave in and the couple quickly made the arrangements and began packing for Italy. Elizabeth hated the thought of leaving her other four children with relatives, but she had no choice. They were too young to make the trip.

Travel by sea in those days was neither safe nor easy. It took seven weeks to journey from New York to Italy. Pirates prowled the Mediterranean, and deadly storms could capsize even the sturdiest of ships.

Fortunately, the weather during their trip was pleasant and Will began to feel a little better. Elizabeth read and rested. She studied the psalms with Anna and watched the reflection of the moon ripple across the water. She wrote in her journal about the breathtaking ocean sunsets. Elizabeth was keeping the journal for Rebecca. She wanted her soul's sister to share in every part of her adventure.

One night, Elizabeth dreamed that she was climbing a steep mountain. She had nearly reached the top when a voice told her, "Never mind, take courage. There is a beautiful green hill on the other side and on it an angel waits for you."

Yet when their ship, *The Shepherdess,* docked in the Leghorn Harbor, Elizabeth found no angel.

Elizabeth's half-brother, Guy Carleton Bayley, who was in Italy at the time, came aboard to greet her. But as Elizabeth excitedly reached to embrace him, Guy abruptly pulled back. Before Guy could explain, a guard appeared out of nowhere.

"Don't touch!" he sternly shouted. "There's an outbreak of yellow fever in New York. Your husband is sick. You will have to be quarantined."

"But he doesn't have yellow fever!" Elizabeth's voice cracked in her panic. "He has consumption. We came here so he could get well!"

"It does not matter," retorted the guard cocking his bayonet. "You and your family will have to be quarantined—for at least a month."

10

THE LAZARETTO

Back in their cabin, Elizabeth heard a welcoming band playing *Hail Columbia*. But the welcome wasn't for the Setons. After seven long weeks of travel, her family wouldn't be going ashore. Elizabeth glanced over at Will. He was deathly pale. She struggled to force back her tears.

Soon a small boat arrived to row the Seton family to the lazaretto, the building farther down the shore where they would be quarantined.

The lazaretto was like a dungeon which overlooked the churning sea. Will, Elizabeth and Anna were led down a shadowy hall to room No. 6. It was dark and damp inside.

"Mommy, I'm afraid!" eight-year-old Anna whimpered.

"It's all right, Anna. Everything will be all right," Elizabeth comforted, giving Anna a hug.

Elizabeth, who had spent months with her father watching immigrants dying at the quarantine station on Staten Island, knew the lazaretto with its musty air and bone-chilling cold was the worst possible environment for Will's inflamed lungs. Yet there was nothing she could do. Mary Filicchi, the wife of Will's friend Filippo, came to greet the Setons, but she was forced to stand on the other side of the fence and could not touch them.

Elizabeth discovered a small closet in their room. She knelt there and prayed, her eyes filling with tears as Will coughed and shivered. It seemed that the day would never end.

One week melted into the next as Elizabeth cared for Will and Anna, and greeted friends who came to see them at the lazaretto. The little family prayed, and that prayer brought them strength and courage.

The captain in charge of the lazaretto was very kind. He sent a servant to cook for and help the Setons. Sometimes he also sent wine and food from his own table to their room.

Elizabeth skipped rope with Anna to keep warm. She listened to Anna's lessons and read Scripture aloud. Some days were brightened by visits from the Filicchis or Guy.

But day by day, Will grew weaker. "My

love, my little ones!" He would gasp. "Father in heaven, thy will be done."

Finally a month had passed. December 19th dawned. It was the day they were to be freed from the lazaretto. Will was still alive.

The door of room No. 6 was unbolted. Two men carried Will to the carriage the Filicchis had sent to bring the family to Pisa. Will gripped Elizabeth's hand as they moved through a small crowd of onlookers.

"Oh, Elizabeth! I feel better," Will murmured weakly once they were on their way. "See there, Anna," he said pointing out the carriage window, "that's the famous Leaning Tower of Pisa."

After a fifteen-mile trip they reached the elegant lodging house provided for them by the Filicchis. Soon a doctor, sent by the Filicchis, also arrived. Four days later Will was feeling so much better that he insisted on going for another carriage ride. With Will propped up on pillows, the Setons rode through the narrow streets of Pisa on a grand tour.

But the next day, Christmas Eve, Will took a turn for the worse. Elizabeth was afraid he wouldn't live until evening.

"How I wish we could have a prayer service," he moaned.

Will gripped Elizabeth's hand
as they moved toward the carriage.

"We can, Will, we can," Elizabeth reassured. She poured a little wine into a glass and prayed some psalms. As they took turns sipping the wine, Elizabeth said, "Let's remember how Jesus suffered for us on the cross. It will give us strength."

On Christmas Day, the captain of *The Shepherdess* visited the Setons in Pisa. At one point in the conversation, Will leaned over and rested his hand on the visitor's. "Please see to it, Captain, that Elizabeth and Anna reach home safely," he said quietly. Captain O'Brien nodded. Elizabeth's heart was pounding. Will was really going to die.

Will's long struggle ended on the morning of December 27, 1803. He died peacefully in Elizabeth's arms, whispering, "My Jesus." He was thirty-five years old.

"It seemed that I loved him more than I could love anyone on earth," Elizabeth wrote many years later.

The next day Elizabeth stood silently by Anna in the tiny English cemetery at Leghorn. Gazing up to the sky she prayed, "My Lord, you are my God. I am now alone in the world with you and my little ones. You are our Father. I place my family in your hands."

11

QUESTIONS

Elizabeth stared at the blank page in front of her. The hand holding her pen was draped in a dark sleeve. She looked down at her simple black dress—the attire of an Italian widow. It felt so strange to be wearing these clothes which constantly reminded her that Will was gone. As if she could ever forget.

Elizabeth drew the paper closer and poised her pen again. How could she possibly tell Rebecca that her brother Will was dead? "My Dear Rebecca," she began. Slowly the words started to flow. But there were so many others who had loved Will. Elizabeth had many more letters to write.

Elizabeth wished that she were home, back in New York. She missed her children. She missed Rebecca. But *The Shepherdess* wasn't ready to sail, and until it was, she and Anna needed a place to stay. Filippo's brother, Antonio Filicchi, and his wife, Amabilia, offered their home.

"Oh, Mama," said Anna coming into the

room, "how many friends God has given us in this new country! They become our friends before they even know us."

"Yes. Thank God for the Filicchis, Anna," Elizabeth responded with a hug, "but most of all, thank God I have you!"

Mother and daughter read together, prayed together and cried together.

"My Papa is praising God in heaven and I shouldn't cry for him," Anna sobbed one day, "but I can't help it, Mama."

"It's good to cry, Anna," Elizabeth comforted. "We both miss Papa very much and our tears are a beautiful sign of love."

The Filicchis were very understanding. Hoping to help Anna and Elizabeth overcome their grief, Mary and Amabilia, the wives of Filippo and Antonio, took them to Florence, one of the cultural centers of Italy. There they attended an opera and visited art galleries, museums and gardens. Twice they even saw the queen. But Anna wasn't very impressed by her royal highness. "She looks just like everyone else," she whispered in surprise.

"That's the way great people should look," Elizabeth whispered back.

Florence was home to many magnificent Catholic churches.

"Would you and Anna like to come to Mass with me tomorrow?" Amabilia asked one Saturday. Elizabeth had never gone to a Catholic Mass before. It had been months since she had stepped inside any church. "Yes," Elizabeth smiled. "We'd love to."

"We will go to the Church of the Annunciation," Amabilia explained. "It is a very ancient and beautiful church."

The next morning found Amabilia, Elizabeth and Anna at Mass, surrounded by hundreds of people kneeling in worship. Elizabeth listened to the fervent hymns and the majestic organ. The music reminded her of heaven. She sank to her knees and cried.

"I've missed being in God's house," she later confided to Mary and Amabilia.

After Mass Elizabeth got a closer look at the church. The gold and silver ornaments, the statues and the detailed, colorful paintings on the walls and ceilings—it was all very different from the plain interior of the churches where she worshipped at home. "It's so beautiful!" Elizabeth exclaimed.

Before she left New York, the Reverend Hobart had prepared Elizabeth for the differences she would encounter in Italy, where most of the people were Catholic. "While Catholics are also Christians," he advised, "I don't want you to come home confused by their different practices and beliefs."

"Don't worry," Elizabeth had replied. "You know how much I love our own faith."

But now, something was happening....

"Pray and inquire, that is all I ask of you," Filippo Filicchi told Elizabeth. Elizabeth trusted Filippo. He was a good friend. So she prayed and asked many questions about the Catholic faith. She found that she liked the Mass. She was especially drawn to the Holy Eucharist. When Amabilia explained to her at Mass one day that Jesus was really present on the altar, Elizabeth wept. *Can this wonderful belief really be true?* She couldn't get the thought out of her mind.

12

HOME AT LAST

Elizabeth continued to write down all of her experiences in the journal she was keeping for Rebecca. By now, all she could think of was home. Baby Bec had been sick when she left for Italy. When Will was dying, he dreamed he saw her in heaven. What if Bec had died? Elizabeth could hardly stand not knowing.

Finally, in February of 1804, *The Shepherdess* was ready to return to America. Elizabeth eagerly led Anna up the ship's gangplank. But the little girl walked slowly and was unusually quiet.

An unexpected storm caused *The Shepherdess* to run into another vessel as it was leaving the harbor that night. The ship was forced to return to port for repairs. All the passengers had to disembark. In the midst of the confusion, Elizabeth noticed Anna's flushed face. She touched her daughter's forehead. "Anna, you're burning!" Elizabeth cried in alarm.

"I feel very sick, Mommy," Anna whispered.

The doctor was immediately called. "It's scarlet fever," he said, shaking his head. "I'm afraid you can't sail. She'll never make the long voyage."

The Filicchis again came to the rescue. They welcomed Elizabeth and Anna back to their home. For three weeks this gracious family dedicatedly nursed "Annina," "little Anna," as they called her in Italian. Elizabeth was touched by their kindness. When Elizabeth became ill and was confined to bed, the family gave her the best care possible. They also lent her books about the Catholic faith to read. Elizabeth discussed these with Filippo and Antonio. She was not yet ready to become a Catholic, even though she wrote to Rebecca, "How happy we would be if we believed what these dear people believe."

In April, another ship bound for New York was leaving Leghorn. The Filicchis booked reservations for Elizabeth and Anna. It was decided that Antonio would accompany them on the long voyage home. It would be safer for the young widow and her daughter not to travel alone. The trip would also give Antonio the chance to check on his business affairs in America and Canada.

Elizabeth visited Will's grave before they set sail. "Good-bye, Will," she whispered through her tears. She knew it was a last farewell, for she would never visit Italy again.

On the voyage home Elizabeth had many things to think about. Antonio let her borrow *The Lives of the Saints* and Elizabeth enjoyed reading about the great heroes and heroines of God. Antonio also explained the Catholic faith to her in more detail and answered her many questions. Together Elizabeth, Anna and Antonio fasted and prayed. Fifty-six days later, they sailed into New York Harbor.

There, waiting on the waterfront as the boat docked were all her children. Elizabeth cried with joy as she hugged them one by one. Even little Bec looked happy and well. Elizabeth scooped her into her arms.

In all the excitement, it was a few minutes before she realized that someone was missing. Where was her "soul's sister"? The happiness of the reunion was shattered when Elizabeth learned that Rebecca, Will's sister, was dying of tuberculosis.

Elizabeth rushed home to Rebecca. All

her dreams of sharing the experiences of Italy and of giving Rebecca the special journal were gone. Rebecca was so weak she could hardly speak. "Oh...Elizabeth...I've ...been...waiting...for...you," she whispered. Elizabeth's eyes filled with tears. "I know, Rebecca, I know you have," she nodded.

Elizabeth cared for Rebecca as if she were her own sister. But barely a month later, Rebecca died. Elizabeth turned more and more to God—the only one who could comfort her, the only one who could give her strength.

13

ALL HIS

It was late, she knew, but Elizabeth wanted to finish writing to her best friend. "God has given me so much to do, Julia. Will's death has left me with no money." She dipped her pen into the ink and brought it back to the paper. "I must somehow find a way to support my children now."

Like the poor widows Elizabeth had helped in the past, she now humbly accepted charity from friends and relatives. Her friend Julia Scott wrote back from Philadelphia offering to adopt Anna and pay for her education. Elizabeth appreciated her generosity, but she refused the offer. It would be too painful to part with Anna.

Elizabeth taught her children at home everyday. At night, they would gather around the fire while she told Bible stories. They sang and danced as Elizabeth played the piano, and before they went to bed, they knelt and said their prayers together. Anna, remembering their time in Italy, wanted them to say the Hail Mary at night. "Teach it to us, Mama," she pleaded. Soon other children in the neighborhood wanted to learn the hymns and prayers and listen to Elizabeth's stories, too.

All during this time, Elizabeth read and prayed and continued to ask God to help her decide whether to become a Catholic. Filippo and Antonio Filicchi often came to New York on business. At each visit they would stop in to see Elizabeth and the family. The Filicchis also wrote to Elizabeth encouraging her to learn more about the Catholic faith. "Try to contact John Carroll, the Catholic bishop of Baltimore. He will help you, Elizabeth," promised Antonio.

At the same time, the Protestant preacher John Hobart was trying to discourage Elizabeth from learning more about Catholicism. Many of her friends would no longer speak to her or even help her with charitable alms. They couldn't understand what she was doing.

Elizabeth was filled with doubts. She grew so thin, her friends were alarmed. She cried all the time. She longed to enter Saint Peter's, the only Catholic church in New York, and worship at the altar, but she was so confused, she feared she might offend

God. At least that's what the Reverend Hobart told her.

Hobart was impatient. Elizabeth was taking too long to decide which religion she wished to live by. As much as it hurt her, Elizabeth knew their friendship was over. That January, after a Sunday service at the Episcopal church, everything suddenly seemed clear to her. She knew which decision was right for her and her children. For the first time in months, Elizabeth felt calm. "I will go peacefully and firmly to the Catholic Church," she resolved.

On Ash Wednesday, February 27, 1805, Elizabeth and her children walked to Saint Peter's Catholic Church. Most of the people there were poor immigrants of Irish, German and French descent. There were stares at first, because Elizabeth was not known in the parish. But soon enough the parishioners welcomed her and her family into their hearts.

Two weeks later, Elizabeth made her profession of faith and was received into the Catholic Church. On March 25th, the day Elizabeth made her First Communion, she joyfully wrote to Amabilia Filicchi, "At last, Amabilia, at last, God is mine and I am all his!"

14

Hurtful Rumors

Saint Peter's Church was crowded. It was really too small for the poor immigrants who filled it every Sunday. People pushed and shoved. Many were dirty and disorderly. Elizabeth had to hold her Bible on her lap so that it wouldn't be stolen. All these things bothered her, but she reminded herself why she was there. She was in God's house. Nothing else mattered.

The situation did matter to Elizabeth's family and friends, though. They were embarrassed that Elizabeth would worship with such people. She was from New York's upper class. She had no business associating with the immigrants they argued.

Antonio Filicchi worried. Elizabeth was a widow with no source of income. She needed the support of her friends and relatives in order to survive. A few of these were trying to understand and help her. Even Elizabeth's stepmother had become friendly again after many years of silence. But how long would it last?

Antonio and Amabilia wrote to Elizabeth suggesting that she move to Italy with her children. Elizabeth didn't feel this was God's plan for her. Instead, she accepted a position as an assistant teacher in a school which was being opened by an English gentleman named Mr. White. Part of the school building would be set aside for living quarters for Elizabeth and her children.

"Now Elizabeth," Mr. White had said, "you may have the position on the condition that you never speak to the children about your religion."

"I've already made that decision, Sir," Elizabeth answered. "I will only teach the assigned subjects."

John Hobart was very upset at the news of Elizabeth's new job. He spread the word that Mr. White was a Catholic and urged parents not to send their children to the school. He told them Elizabeth would surely try to make Catholics out of the students.

This was anything but true. Mr. White and his family were good Protestants and Elizabeth was not bringing her religious beliefs into the classroom. Some of Elizabeth's close friends who had heard the rumors went to speak with Hobart. When he realized he was wrong, he tried to take back the false things he had said about Mr. White's school. But it was too late. When the school opened in May, there were only three students besides the Seton and White children. By July, Mr. White could no longer pay the rent. The school closed and Elizabeth and her family were without a home.

Once again Elizabeth's sister Mary and her husband Dr. Post took them in. Elizabeth was very grateful to Mary and Wright, but she felt guilty that they had to squeeze six extra people into their house in Greenwich Village. Besides that, Saint Peter's was too far away for her and the children to walk to Mass on Sundays.

The Posts' friends liked to discuss religion with Elizabeth. They never seemed to have anything good to say about Catholics, but Elizabeth would listen patiently. "Come hear our fine preachers," they would urge her.

Elizabeth's children heard mean things about their new faith, too. Many times their friends made fun of them because they had joined the Catholic Church with their mother.

When the school opened, there were only three students besides the Seton and White children.

In November Elizabeth was relieved when she found a job as an assistant at a school. The headmaster was an Episcopalian minister. He hired her to do the cooking, cleaning and sewing for a dozen boys who would live in her home. Elizabeth awoke every morning before the sun rose. Many nights she fell asleep saying her evening prayers. But she liked the hard work. She was happy to be in charge of her household once again. Her children were happy, too.

William was now nine years old. Richard was seven. Elizabeth wanted to enroll them in a Catholic school.

"Antonio," she wrote, "when you come back to the United States, could you please find a good school for the boys? Your generous offering to pay for their education is a blessing from God. It's more than I would dream of asking, but I have no idea where to enroll the boys."

Antonio visited schools from Montreal to Maryland, gathering information for Elizabeth. When he came to visit her, Elizabeth chose Georgetown College in Maryland.

"Bishop Carroll of Baltimore is an old friend of mine," Antonio reminded Elizabeth before he left. "See if you can contact him. He often visits Georgetown College and I'm sure he will keep a good watch over your sons."

Elizabeth followed Antonio's advice. Bishop Carroll was to become her good friend, too. Whenever he met William and Richard at the school, he wrote to reassure Elizabeth that they were doing well. He knew how much she missed them.

15

PERSECUTION

Richard and William weren't the only children Elizabeth missed. She often thought of Will's younger sisters who had left her home when Will lost his business.

Sixteen-year-old Cecilia Seton now lived with her brother, James. Cecilia had tuberculosis. Elizabeth prayed for her every day. "I still think of you as my daughter," she wrote to Cecilia. "I wish you were here with me."

Cecilia longed to become a Catholic. Her older sister Harriet had tried learning about the Catholic faith, too. But when her relatives found out and got upset, Harriet gave up.

Cecilia, instead, never did. One day, when she was visiting her sister's home, she broke the news. "I've made up my mind, Charlotte. I'm going to join the Catholic Church."

Charlotte was furious. "What? How dare you even mention the word in this house! This is all Elizabeth's fault."

"No, Charlotte. It's my own idea."

"I don't believe a word of it! You've been listening to that traitor.... I'll see to it that Elizabeth is thrown out of New York State. She'll be begging bread on the streets when I'm finished with her. Remember, my husband is a member of the state legislature. He has the power to send her away."

Cecilia was locked in her room for days. The family hoped she would change her mind. She didn't. Now they were even angrier.

"We'll burn Elizabeth's house down," Charlotte fumed. "As for you, we'll get you a one way ticket to the West Indies. The ship is already waiting in the harbor. Pack your things, Cecilia!"

Cecilia calmly packed her clothes and left the house. She went to live with Elizabeth. Three days later she was received into the Catholic Church.

Now Elizabeth's family and friends were enraged. "You're to blame for Cecilia's decision, Elizabeth," they accused.

"You will inherit nothing from me," Elizabeth's wealthy uncle angrily wrote. "I'm hereby removing you from my will."

Elizabeth's well-to-do godmother did the same. John Hobart personally visited all Elizabeth's friends and told them to stay away from her. The school children in Elizabeth's home lost respect for her and became disobedient. Even one of Elizabeth's best friends stopped speaking with her.

Other troubles were also brewing. That Christmas Eve, a mob of fifty men gathered outside Saint Peter's Church. They tried to stop the Mass and tear down the church. On Christmas morning, a brutal fight broke out and a city official was killed trying to defend the church. The riot only ended when the mayor appeared on the scene and ordered that Catholics were not to be harassed.

Now it was very clear to Elizabeth how the people of New York felt about Catholics. What if something happened to her? Who would take care of her children? She wondered.

16

AN INVITATION

Elizabeth loved it when she returned from an errand and Anna, Kit or Bec playfully threw themselves into her arms. She wanted to have this same loving relationship with God. "I want to try to please God as you try to please me," Elizabeth told Kit one day. "I want to obey his voice as you obey mine. I want to run with joy to meet God as you always run to meet me."

As a mother, Elizabeth felt a special love for the Virgin Mary. When she was confirmed, she chose to add the name Mary to her own. After that, Elizabeth would often sign her letters, "Mrs. M. E. A. Seton."

By spring of 1808, Elizabeth had moved her family to a smaller home. There were fewer school children living with them and she barely had enough money to pay the rent. When Father Dubourg, a priest friend she had met a few years earlier, brought William and Richard up from Baltimore for a visit, he was saddened to see Elizabeth's situation.

"You can't stay here, Elizabeth," he finally said. "I think I have a solution. We need someone to begin a school for girls in Baltimore. You would be close to Richard and William and the atmosphere would be good for your other children." He paused. "Catholics are not treated badly in Maryland as they are here in New York."

Elizabeth thought and prayed and asked for advice. Within a few weeks she made up her mind. She would move to Baltimore.

On June 9, Elizabeth and her three daughters gathered on the wharf, their bags piled around them. They boarded the *Grand Sachem* which would take them to Maryland.

Elizabeth stood on deck as the ship sailed out of the harbor. She watched as they glided past her former home on the Battery. How many nights she had searched for the light of Rebecca's lantern shining through its windows. Just ahead of them was Staten Island. How she wished she could have visited her father's grave one last time. Tears welled up in her eyes as she thought of her father and all he had done for the poor immigrants. But soon New York's skyline was behind them.

One week later, Elizabeth, Anna, Kit and Bec stepped off the dock in Baltimore, Maryland. It was raining steadily. They took a carriage to Saint Mary's Seminary.

The first Mass at the seminary's new chapel was being celebrated that morning. Elizabeth and her daughters arrived just after the Mass had begun. As they stepped inside the chapel, they were greeted by the soaring music of the organ and choir. The chapel was ablaze with candles. The scent of freshly cut flowers filled the air. Elizabeth recognized the voice leading the prayers. It was her good friend Father Hurley. Elizabeth fell to her knees. She was sure she had never heard or seen anything so beautiful.

After Mass, Elizabeth and the children shared a happy reunion with Archbishop Carroll, Father Dubourg and Father Hurley.

"I can't believe so many people are being nice to us," Anna beamed.

"Maryland is a state where many Catholics live. Did you know that, Anna?" Father Dubourg smiled. "It was the first state in the Union to allow Catholics to freely practice their religion," he proudly explained.

"Elizabeth," Archbishop Carroll said, "Let us take you to the house where you will be living and teaching. I think it will be to your liking."

Elizabeth smiled. She was home.

17

Beginnings

All summer long, Elizabeth entertained many important people from Baltimore who came to visit her little house on Paca Street.

In the fall, the school opened. There were seven students in all—Elizabeth's three daughters and four other young girls who boarded at the house. William and Richard lived nearby at Saint Mary's College.

The school day began in the chapel at six in the morning and ended there again at six-thirty in the evening. Elizabeth taught arithmetic, reading, English, French and needlework. After classes she needed to study the material she would be teaching the next day. "At night I stuff my head with mathematics, dollar signs, decimals and everything a student, not a teacher, should be learning," she wrote jokingly to her friend Julia. "I never thought I'd be studying all of this at thirty-five!"

Elizabeth loved to teach. She had secretly dreamed of living in a convent and being a teaching assistant. But Father Dubourg had much greater plans for her. He wanted to form students from the Paca Street School into a new congregation of religious sisters. And he wanted Elizabeth to be its foundress!

"Elizabeth, you will become the mother of many daughters," he promised.

A sister? A foundress? Where was God leading her? Elizabeth didn't know. She was ready to follow, but an important question troubled her.

"What about my children, Father?" she asked. "Before anything else I'm a mother, and I always will be."

"Don't worry Elizabeth," the priest responded. "Just have trust. If this is something God wants, he'll take care of everything."

On October 6, Elizabeth wrote enthusiastically to Cecilia Seton, telling her all about the plan for a new congregation of teaching sisters. "Try to come to Baltimore as soon as possible," she urged.

Another Cecilia, Cecilia O'Conway, became the first young woman to join Elizabeth in a life dedicated to God. She arrived in Baltimore from Philadelphia on December 7, 1808.

One big problem remained. A new congregation of sisters couldn't be started without money. And Elizabeth had none. She wrote to Filippo and Antonio Filicchi, asking if they might be able to help. Actually, Antonio had written to her in November, promising financial help. But Napoleon and his armies were marching across Europe at that time and most of the ports were closed to foreign ships. It took an entire year for the letter to reach Elizabeth.

In the meantime, Elizabeth prayed hard. "Please, God, make your will clear to me. I don't understand what you want."

Elizabeth had met Samuel Cooper, a seminarian at Saint Mary's. He and Elizabeth had become friends, but Mr. Cooper didn't know about the plans for the new community of sisters.

Mr. Cooper was wealthy. He needed to give his fortune away before he could be ordained a priest. Hoping that his money could be used to build a Catholic school for girls, he decided to speak with Father Dubourg about his idea.

Father listened carefully. "Samuel," he finally asked, "do you know Mrs. Seton?"

"Yes. Yes, I do. Why do you ask, Father?"

"Because she's trying to begin a new congregation of sisters to teach young girls, and has not a cent," the priest explained.

"Perhaps God wishes you to use your money to help her."

Mr. Cooper happily agreed. He soon purchased land for the new community and school in Emmitsburg, a town about fifty miles outside of Baltimore. A small building already stood on the property. It would be used for the convent and school until a larger house could be built.

Elizabeth could only smile. Yes, God was providing.

18

MOTHER SETON

"....And I bless you in the name of the Father and of the Son and of the Holy Spirit. Amen." Archbishop Carroll raised his hand in the sign of the cross over Elizabeth. Elizabeth blessed herself. *I am yours, Jesus,* she prayed in her heart, *all yours.*

It was the Feast of the Annunciation, March 25, 1809. Elizabeth had just pronounced her vows of poverty, chastity and obedience for one year. She was now a sister. From that day on she would be known as Mother Seton.

Everyone called Elizabeth "Mother," even people who didn't know her. Elizabeth had answered to many names in her life— Betty, Betsy, Elizabeth and Eliza. But "Mother," was her favorite name of all.

That spring, three more young women came to Baltimore to join Elizabeth and Cecilia O'Conway in the new community. On June 1, 1809, the five women put on black dresses and ruffled caps. This would be their religious habit for the rest of their lives. Elizabeth had worn such an outfit since Will's death in Italy. But now she added something to it. Wrapped around the leather belt of her habit was a large rosary, the symbol of her favorite prayer to the Mother of God.

That night, thinking of her sinfulness and imperfection, Elizabeth fell to the floor and sobbed. "O God, I'm unfit for the task which you are entrusting to me," she prayed. "But because it is your wish, I will try. I promise to try my hardest."

It hadn't taken long for Cecilia Seton's relatives in New York to forgive her for becoming a Catholic. They had forgiven Elizabeth, too. So Cecilia had gone back to live with her brother, James. Now Cecilia wanted to join Elizabeth and the new congregation. For months she had tried to leave New York, but always without success. Finally the time was right.

Harriet Seton accompanied her sister Cecilia to Baltimore in the middle of June. Elizabeth, Anna, Kit and Bec were so excited to see her again. "The doctors say she needs fresh air because of her tuberculosis," Harriet confided to Elizabeth.

"Then we should leave right away for

Emmitsburg," Elizabeth decided. "The mountain air will be perfect."

On June 21, Elizabeth, Anna, Cecilia, Harriet and Maria, one of the first sisters, set out for Emmitsburg. The rest of the little group of sisters remained in Baltimore.

The fifty-mile journey along rough roads was a difficult one. The Maryland summer was sticky and the air was heavy and thick. Except for Cecilia, the women walked beside the wagon and led their horses along the stony paths.

As they approached the blue-green mountains, the trail grew steeper. It wound past creeks and huge mounds of rock. The tallest peak, Saint Mary's Mountain, loomed before them. At its base, stood the tiny log church also called Saint Mary's. A second small church, Saint Joseph's, was located in the town of Emmitsburg. The pastor there was Father John Dubois. This kind priest had agreed to move out of his house and let the sisters live there until their own home was ready.

At the end of July, repairs to the building on the sisters' property were completed. The sisters named it the Stone House. A few days later, Sister Rose White arrived with the rest of the sisters from Baltimore. They brought with them William and Richard and two students from the Paca Street School. With nine more people, the Stone House was already too crowded.

Father Dubourg came unexpectedly that day, too. He looked around then quietly walked out of the house. Elizabeth followed him.

"Father, where are you going?" she asked in surprise.

"Mother," he smiled, "there aren't even enough cups and saucers for supper this evening. I'm going to town to buy some."

The next morning after Mass, the community's officers were announced. Sister Rose was the oldest and also more experienced than the others. She would be Elizabeth's assistant. Sister Kitty was named housekeeper. Sister Cecilia Seton was appointed as secretary and teacher. And Sister Sally would serve as treasurer. The little community was taking its first steps.

19

EARLY DAYS

School would only start in the fall, but already the days were busy. The sisters rose at five in the morning to pray before Mass. On their way to church and back, they prayed the rosary. There were also daily times set aside for prayer, reading and recreation.

"Mother," Father Dubourg suggested one day, "you and the sisters should choose a place for your cemetery."

The sisters took a walk together through the woods that evening. Harriet, who was with them, was eating an apple. She jokingly tossed the core against an enormous oak tree. "That marks my spot!" she laughed.

"We'll remember, Harriet," everyone teased in return.

Some chores like doing the laundry took the whole day. The clothes had to be hauled in heavy wash tubs down the hill to Toms Creek. There the sisters stood for hours in icy water until their fingers and feet were shriveled and numb. In the winter it was even worse. The ice and snow caused their skin to chafe and bleed.

In their little garden the sisters grew carrots which they used to make coffee. They slept with their mattresses crowded together on the floor because there were no beds.

A few hundred yards away from the Stone House, a larger building was being constructed. It would serve as both school and convent.

William and Richard now lived and studied nearby at Mount Saint Mary's College. Every Wednesday they came to spend the evening with their family.

Harriet Seton loved living in the community of the sisters. One moonlit summer night as she and Elizabeth were taking a walk, Harriet suddenly burst out, "I've decided to become a Catholic, Elizabeth."

"What will your relatives say?" gasped Elizabeth.

"It doesn't matter what they say. Instead of going back to New York, I want to stay here at the convent and work with you."

"If you believe this is God's will, Harriet," Elizabeth said softly, "then may it be done."

In November, Archbishop Carroll made his first visit to the sisters at Emmitsburg. At the altar in a little corner of the Stone House he confirmed Harriet and Anna.

One month later, Harriet fell deathly sick with a high fever. After weeks of suffering, she died just before Christmas. The sisters, remembering the big oak tree she wanted to be buried under, placed her there as the first in their cemetery. Elizabeth felt that she had lost a daughter.

Several members of the community became seriously ill that Christmas. The bitter mountain wind sneaked in through the cracks and crevices of the Stone House. Sometimes snow drifted through the roof, blanketing the sisters who were sleeping upstairs.

With the arrival of two more women, the Stone House could no longer accommodate everyone. Sisters Rose, Kitty and Susan had to move into the unfinished house up the hill. It was so cold that they sat at their spinning wheels most of the day, pedaling feverishly just to keep warm. When it rained, the path between the two houses became a trail of deep mud that had to be waded through. Because they had no clock, the sisters in the house still under construction sometimes rushed over to the Stone House for morning prayers—in the middle of the night!

On February 20, 1810, all the sisters joined Sister Rose, Sister Susan and Sister Kitty in the new house which they called the White House. The building wasn't finished yet, and the wet plaster and wood chips attracted fleas which bit the sisters until their skin turned purple. One day a storm caused the temporary kitchen to cave in. A cascade of rain came down the chimney, and Sister Rose was forced to serve a very soggy supper that night.

On Sundays, the sisters walked up the mountain to Mass. They scrambled over fences and skipped from stone to stone across the creek on their way through the woods. When it rained, the creek swelled, and they had to cross it one at a time on the back of their old horse. Without umbrellas or shawls, their clothes would be soaked all the way through and their shoes caked with mud. But they never complained. Everything was for God. And they were happy.

*The sisters scrambled over fences
and skipped from stone to stone across
the creek on their way to Mass.*

20

MORE OF THE CROSS

On February 22, 1810, three Catholic children from Emmitsburg were enrolled at the sisters' school, which they named "Saint Joseph's." These children would go down in history as the first parochial school students in America.

But not everything was going well. By the beginning of April, Sister Cecilia Seton was so sick that Elizabeth and Sister Susan had to take her to Baltimore for medical care.

"I'm afraid she's already in the last stages of tuberculosis," the doctor told Elizabeth. "There is nothing I can do except try to make her comfortable. I suggest that you stay here in the city and not make Sister endure the ride back to Emmitsburg."

Sister Cecilia died on April 29 in Elizabeth's arms. Elizabeth and Sister Susan made the sad journey back to Emmitsburg to bury her.

Cecilia was laid beside her sister Harriet in the community's tiny cemetery. She became the first of many sisters to be buried there. Elizabeth's friends knew how much she had loved Cecilia and they tried to comfort her. But Elizabeth's greatest consoler was the Lord. She accepted the cross he offered her with love.

As Mother Superior, it was Elizabeth's duty to help the other sisters through their sadness and encourage and take care of them when they were sick or tired, cold or hungry. Most of all, Elizabeth made sure the sisters continued to grow closer to God. Even though she had so much to do during the day, prayer always came first for Elizabeth and she taught her sisters by her good example.

Elizabeth prayed for God's help with the difficult tasks she was often called upon to do—whether it was to settle an argument among the children, solve a problem for the sisters, or find money she didn't have to pay an unexpected bill. God was always her "loving Father" and she trusted him in everything.

Saint Joseph's School was soon filled and more children were waiting to enroll as soon as there was space.

"Mother Seton would take in the whole

county if she could!" Father Dubois once exclaimed to Archbishop Carroll.

Elizabeth served as the school's principal as well as a teacher. She also gave lessons to some of the boys at Mount Saint Mary's. Elizabeth translated important documents from French into English and sometimes even helped priests prepare their sermons. All this work was very tiring for her and she would often write letters to her friends "with one eye open and the other closed."

"Mother, you really shouldn't work so hard," Sister Rose would say with concern. "Please, let me help you with some of your duties."

Elizabeth would only smile and pat Sister Rose's hand. "I love my work so much, Rose, that I don't feel rushed or too busy. Not at all. Not at all."

21

Sisters of Charity

Soon after Elizabeth became Mother Superior, Father Dubourg wrote her a letter from Baltimore. In it he directed Elizabeth and the sisters to have nothing more to do with Father Babade, a priest who used to hear the confessions of the sisters and give them spiritual guidance.

This suggestion upset Elizabeth and her sisters. Father Dubourg, in turn, became angry at their reaction and resigned as chaplain and priest superior. After several months, Father David was appointed to take Father Dubourg's place. Unfortunately, he and Elizabeth didn't see eye to eye on many things. Father David wanted Sister Rose to be Mother Superior and he let everyone, including the archbishop, know it.

The sisters wanted Elizabeth to be in charge of the community. So did Archbishop Carroll.

For a long time Elizabeth didn't know what would happen. She felt very confused and alone. She waited and tried her best to keep calm. "Whatever happens is God's will for us," she quietly reminded the sisters. "Remember, we are his now. He is our Shepherd."

In the end, Archbishop Carroll sent Father David away and Elizabeth stayed, to the joy of all her sisters.

"Truly, Mother, your good work is affecting the lives of many people," the archbishop remarked to Elizabeth one day.

"Thank you, Your Excellency, but one thing still bothers me," Elizabeth replied, lowering her eyes.

"And what is that?"

"I will always be a mother to my five children, Your Excellency. If it ever comes to the point that I must give them up for the good of the congregation, then—" Elizabeth's voice dropped to a whisper, "then I can sincerely tell you, I will give up the congregation. I must be a mother to my own children first of all."

"And you will be, Mother Seton," the archbishop smiled.

The sisters had begun calling themselves the "Sisters of Charity." They took their name from the French community founded in 1633 by Saint Vincent de Paul. From the beginning the sisters had adopted many of the regulations and ideas of the French Order. Now it was time to choose permanent rules for their community at Emmitsburg.

Should they follow all the rules of Saint Vincent's sisters in France? Elizabeth placed the decision in God's hands. She knew that the French rules might require her to be separated from her children. If so, Elizabeth had decided to resign as Mother Superior. Again, she repeated to the archbishop, "The only answer I have to every question is: 'I am a mother.'"

On September 11, 1811, Archbishop Carroll approved the rules of the Sisters of Charity of Saint Joseph in Emmitsburg. They were similar to those of the French sisters, but they had been modified to allow Elizabeth to keep her children and remain as Mother Superior.

As a young woman, Elizabeth had been called a "Protestant Sister of Charity." Now, she truly *was* a Sister of Charity.

22

ANNA

Elizabeth and Anna guided their horses slowly along the steep mountain ridge. The autumn breeze felt cool and refreshing. Below them, sheep and children dotted the grassy meadow.

Anna pointed to the valley. "Look, Mother! Have you ever seen such a precious sight?"

Elizabeth turned toward Anna and smiled. The brilliant fall colors were fading now. And she couldn't help noticing that the light in Anna's eyes was fading, too. A month earlier, tuberculosis, the plague of the Seton family, had announced its sorrowful return. Elizabeth knew that her oldest daughter was dying.

Whenever Anna was well enough, Elizabeth liked to take her horseback riding. Anna loved this rare time alone with her mother. They laughed and talked about everything. About the times when Anna had been angry with Elizabeth. About the boyfriend who had hurt Anna so badly when he decided to marry someone else. They talked about God and friends and school. They even talked about Anna's dying.

By Christmas, Anna was suffering greatly. She grew so thin that her bones stuck out in places. Elizabeth tried to be strong, but her very soul was torn to see her daughter in so much pain.

Sometimes Elizabeth would go to a corner of the little chapel and sob. Anna noticed her mother's tears one day. "Are you crying for me?" she asked softly, stroking her mother's damp cheek. "Don't, Mother. I'll spend a happy forever with God and with you. What a beautiful thought! Don't cry anymore."

"Are you afraid to die, Anna?" Elizabeth whispered.

"No, Mother," Anna smiled. "I'm not afraid."

Before she died, Anna made an important decision. "Mother, I want to become a Sister of Charity."

"Are you sure?"

"Yes," Anna nodded, "it's what I want more than anything else."

On January 30, 1812, Father Dubois administered the Anointing of the Sick to Anna and she received Holy Communion.

There was only one thing left to do. The next day, Anna pronounced her vows as a Sister of Charity.

"Now it's done.... Now I belong entirely to God!" she exclaimed joyfully.

Anna lingered on a few more months. On March 12, 1812, like Harriet and Cecilia, she died peacefully in Elizabeth's arms. She was only sixteen years old.

Elizabeth had already lost her mother and father. She had lost Will. She had lost brothers and sisters and Rebecca and Harriet and Cecilia. But Anna's death seemed to be more than she could bear.

Anna had always been there for Elizabeth, lending her quiet strength and courage when her mother had overwhelming trials to face. Anna had always understood. And now Anna was gone. Elizabeth pressed her folded hands to her forehead and wept. "Father, thy will be done," she repeated, "in everything."

23

THE SECRET

Months passed before Elizabeth could feel any joy again. She finally began going through Anna's things. On her music and books, even on the walls of her bedroom Anna had written one word over and over again— "Eternity." Elizabeth had to smile.

That May, Mary and Wright Post came from New York to visit. It had been four years since Elizabeth had seen her sister and brother-in-law.

Mary sat on the bed where Anna had died and cried. "Elizabeth, I'm so glad I came to Emmitsburg," she finally managed to say. "It's so peaceful. I see now why Anna was very happy here. And I can't believe all the work you and your sisters are doing! You're performing miracles! Twenty sisters and fifty students. Elizabeth, what's your secret?"

Elizabeth smiled and shrugged her thin shoulders. "Love," she said simply. "We just love. We've managed, so far, to always have something on the table, but our school must also begin to support itself." Elizabeth's dark eyes grew serious. "Many of our students are poor and can pay nothing for their education. Others pay with the produce of their farms, like chickens, eggs, or even a calf, now and then. I've decided to also begin admitting students from families who can afford to pay tuition. This should help to cover some of our biggest expenses."

"God has brought you this far. He won't abandon you now," Mary reassured, giving her sister a hug.

"I know he won't," Elizabeth replied softly.

Elizabeth loved her students. She sent them notes to encourage them to pray and to remind them that they were in her prayers.

"Mother Seton, are we all going to grow up to be sisters?" a little student with big, worried eyes asked one day.

Elizabeth cupped the tiny face in her hands and smiled. "I don't think so, my dear. God will be very happy with whatever you decide to be when you grow up, as long as you always try to love and please him."

"That's good!" exclaimed the girl in relief, "because I'm not even Catholic!"

Years after the girls left the sisters'

school, they kept in close touch with their "Mother." They wrote asking her advice on dating, marriage, prayer, cooking, and dozens of other things. Although her schedule was very busy, Elizabeth always found time to answer each letter.

The community of sisters continued to grow. One day Elizabeth received a letter from Father Hurley, her friend in Philadelphia. She began reading aloud to the sisters: "What I am asking, Mother, is if you can send some sisters to take over the orphanage here. There's a great need." Elizabeth looked up at the eager young faces surrounding her. "What do you think?" she questioned. There was no need to ask twice. Such squeals of excitement filled the room that even Elizabeth was surprised. The sisters had always dreamed of staffing an orphanage. But they never thought the opportunity would come so soon.

24

JOYS AND SORROWS

"Good-bye!"

"Write soon!"

"Our prayers go with you!"

The sisters, clustered around the front door of the White House on that September morning in 1814, tearfully watched and waved as the carriage pulled away. Sisters Rose, Susan and Teresa, wrapped in the new flannel shawls Elizabeth had given them, waved back from the carriage windows until the White House disappeared from view. They were on their way to Philadelphia and the orphanage.

It was a frightening time for the women to travel. America and England were at war. The city of Washington had just been burned and the British had attacked Fort McHenry in Baltimore. Through it all the sisters passed safely and arrived in Philadelphia.

What they found there was near tragedy. The existing orphanage, which they named

"Saint Joseph's," was five thousand dollars in debt. There was very little to eat. The sisters made coffee out of dried corn, but couldn't afford to buy sugar to sweeten it. They continued to pray and work hard, though, and Sister Rose managed the finances so well that by the end of the second year, they had *extra* money and could take in more children.

Two years before the Sisters of Charity had established themselves in Philadelphia, Elizabeth's ten-year-old daughter Rebecca had fallen on the ice and injured her hip. The pain continued for months and Bec became lame. Elizabeth sent her to see Dr. Chatard, a respected doctor and Elizabeth's friend. He concluded that Bec would never regain the use of her leg, but that the pain would eventually disappear. It didn't.

Three years later, a tumor formed on Bec's leg. This time Elizabeth had her examined by a specialist in Philadelphia. Bec stayed with the sisters at Saint Joseph's Orphanage. Elizabeth, knowing how frightened Bec must feel to be so far from home, wrote to her every day.

Elizabeth's close friend Julia Scott also lived in Philadelphia. She was happy to do what she could for Bec. Julia took Bec to see the historic sights of Philadelphia: Independence Hall, the Liberty Bell, the museums. The thirteen-year-old enjoyed it all.

Elizabeth had hoped and prayed that the doctor could do something to help Bec. But it was too late. Just like her father and her sister Anna, just like so many of her Seton relatives, Bec had tuberculosis. It had formed in the tumor on her leg.

Bec made the long, journey back to Emmitsburg. She was in constant pain. It hurt her to stand or to lie down. Back at the convent, she leaned against Elizabeth's side day and night, spending her time reading or drawing.

"My Dear Julia," Elizabeth wrote to her friend, "I am writing while little Bec is sitting on my lap. She hardly ever leaves me now, even for a second. Father Bruté comes often and draws cartoons to cheer her up. We often speak of you, and of the wonderful times she had with you in Philadelphia."

Months passed. Because of Bec's constant weight, Elizabeth began to walk with a limp and her arm grew numb. Kit took over most of her secretarial work.

"I'm going to die soon, Mother," Bec told

Elizabeth one night. "I've dreamed that I've just been handing Jesus my little cup. It's all full. I know he's coming for me."

Elizabeth was holding fourteen-year-old Bec in her arms when she died a few hours later on November 3, 1816.

Bec died in Elizabeth's arms.

25

WITH THE FATHER

Accepting Bec's death was not like the struggle Elizabeth had suffered when Anna died, and she wrote to Julia, "With God to help me, I can face anything."

Elizabeth was now forty-four years old and weak and frail with tuberculosis herself. She knew that she would not live much longer and she prepared herself for eternity day by day.

Richard now lived in Italy, working at the Filicchis' counting house. William was in the Navy. Elizabeth missed her sons very much. She was always writing to them, but they hardly ever wrote back.

One day, Elizabeth finally received a letter from William. He wrote from Boston.

"I'm leaving on a two-year voyage to the Pacific, Mother. How is your health? If you're not well, I'd like to come and visit you before I sail."

Elizabeth realized it would be difficult for William to leave her if he saw how sick she really was, so she reassured him that her illness was nothing serious. But deep in her heart Elizabeth knew she wouldn't live another two years. She knew she would never see William again.

On the way down the coast, William's ship was rocked by a terrible storm. As he slept in his hammock, he dreamed that Elizabeth stood before him. "Are you prepared, my William?" she asked him.

William awoke with a start to find himself knee-deep in water. The ship was sinking! When it docked in Virginia for emergency repairs, William was given leave to visit his mother. Elizabeth was more than grateful for this chance to say goodbye. Eight days later, William sailed for the Pacific.

By now, Elizabeth had developed the deep, harsh cough of tuberculosis. It never left her. She could hardly swallow or eat and she always felt tired. But she didn't stop working. Carpenters were constructing a new building at the convent. Elizabeth climbed up on a high pile of boards to inspect their work. The sharp wind pierced her thin body. Within a few days, she came down with a high fever.

"I will not get well, not this time," she told the sisters who gathered around her.

Elizabeth drew all her strength from Jesus in the Holy Eucharist. The sisters placed her bed in a small room adjoining the chapel so she could participate at Mass everyday without having to get up.

In those days, Catholics were required to fast from all food and drink from twelve midnight until Mass the next morning in order to receive Holy Communion. One night, Elizabeth was so thirsty that she could hardly stand it. The sisters offered her water to relieve her suffering, but Elizabeth refused to take it. When Father Bruté brought her Holy Communion in the morning, Elizabeth started to sob.

"Peace, Mother," Father said softly. "Are you in pain?"

Elizabeth raised her head. "No! No! Only give me Jesus!" she begged through her tears. She had been crying for joy.

On January 2, 1821, Father Dubois administered the Anointing of the Sick to Elizabeth while all the sisters knelt around her bed and recited the prayers for the dying. She looked from one to the other and smiled.

"Thank you, Sisters, for being kind enough to stay with me during my sufferings," she said in a weak voice. "Be children of the Church!" she struggled to add. "Be children of the Church!"

The early morning hours of January 4 found several of the sisters praying and keeping watch at Elizabeth's bedside. All of a sudden, Elizabeth herself began a prayer which had become one of her favorites: "May the most just, the most high and the most amiable will of God be in all things fulfilled, praised and exalted above all forever."

Then, one of the sisters who knew how much Elizabeth loved French, leaned closer to the bed and began praying softly in that language. Elizabeth smiled. The last words she whispered were, "Jesus...Mary...Joseph." A little while later she peacefully passed into eternity. She was finally home with her heavenly Father.

26

MIRACLES

On a crisp autumn day in 1963, a construction worker named Carl Kalin lay dying in a New York hospital. He was suffering from a brain infection and his doctors had given up all hope of his recovery.

Day by day, Mr. Kalin grew steadily worse. His face turned purple and his whole body shook with convulsions. The doctor on duty passed the medical chart back to the nurse. "He probably won't last the night," he predicted.

One of the Sisters of Charity who worked at the hospital was called to comfort Carl's wife. The sister took Mrs. Kalin to the next room and together they prayed.

"Let's begin a novena of prayers in honor of Mother Elizabeth Seton," the sister suggested. "If it's God's will, maybe your husband will be healed through her intercession."

Soon other sisters from the hospital joined in the novena for the dying man.

Two weeks later, Mr. Kalin walked out of

the hospital completely cured. The Catholic Church proclaimed his cure a miracle.

But it wasn't the only one. In Baltimore, a young girl was healed of leukemia after prayers were offered to Mother Seton. And a sister in Louisiana recovered from liver cancer through Mother Seton's intercession. These healings too were carefully recorded by the Church.

Twelve years after his cure, Carl Kalin joined 20,000 other Americans in Saint Peter's Square in Rome. It was September 14, 1975. Americans everywhere were getting ready to celebrate the two hundredth birthday of the United States with parades and fireworks. Pope Paul VI gave them one more reason to celebrate on that sunny Roman morning.

"Elizabeth Ann Bayley Seton is a saint!" his voice rang out over the excited crowd packing Saint Peter's Square. "Rejoice, we say to the great nation of the United States of America. Rejoice for your glorious daughter!"

When Elizabeth Seton died at the age of forty-six, she had been a Catholic for only fifteen years. She left behind fifty sisters in three growing communities of the Sisters of Charity.

Today, more than 5,000 of Mother Seton's daughters continue to carry out her good works throughout North America. Some operate hospitals, like the one in which Mr. Kalin was miraculously cured. Others teach in schools, care for the homeless and serve the elderly.

Elizabeth's children remembered her example, too. Richard Seton died at sea at the age of twenty-five, while nursing an Episcopalian minister back to health. Fun-loving Kit eventually joined the Sisters of Mercy. And William raised a daughter who became a sister and a son who became an archbishop.

When Elizabeth lived there, New York City had only one small Catholic Church. Today it has hundreds. Elizabeth's old home on State Street, now a shrine, is counted among them.

New York's beautiful cathedral, Saint Patrick's, also has a shrine honoring Mother Seton. An inscription on the cathedral's bronze doors proudly proclaims: "Mother Elizabeth Seton—Daughter of New York."

We celebrate Mother Seton's feast day on January 4.

PRAYER

Saint Elizabeth Ann, you served God in many wonderful ways. You were a wife, a mother, a widow, a foundress and a sister—all in one lifetime!

Your love for God and his people made you strong and courageous. Because you loved so much, you also had the honor of being named the first American-born saint.

Thank you for the special help you gave to children and the poor. Thank you for beginning a congregation of sisters to continue your good work.

Help me to love, no matter what. I want to follow Jesus as you did. Pray for me, Mother Seton.

Amen.

GLOSSARY

1. Anointing of the Sick—the sacrament by which Jesus gives spiritual comfort and strength, and sometimes physical help, to someone who is dangerously ill due to sickness, injury or old age.

2. Chaplain—a priest who ministers to a certain group of people.

3. Congregation (religious)—a community of men or women who live together and make vows of chastity, poverty and obedience to God. The members of a congregation share a life of prayer and carry out special works of service for the good of God's people.

4. Delirious—in a condition of extreme mental agitation characterized by restlessness, confusion, and even hallucinations. This state is often brought on by a high fever.

5. Foundress—a woman who begins a religious congregation or order.

6. Novena—nine days of prayer for some special need or occasion. This custom recalls the time that Mary and the first disciples of Jesus spent praying together between the ascension of Jesus into heaven and the coming of the Holy Spirit on Pentecost.

7. Parochial school—a school that belongs to and is supported by a parish.

8. Quarantine—to isolate or set apart from everyone else a person who is believed to have a contagious disease, so as to keep the disease from spreading.

9. Shrine—a holy place where people come to honor Jesus, Mary or one of the saints.

10. Vows—special promises made to God. Members of a religious congregation or Order make the vows of chastity, poverty and obedience.

Daughters of St. Paul

| We Pray | We Preach | We Praise |

Centering our lives on Jesus, Way, Truth, Life

Witnessing to the joy of living totally for Jesus

Sharing Jesus with people through various forms of media: books, music, video, & multimedia

If you would like more information on following Jesus and spreading His Gospel

as a Daughter of St. Paul…

contact:

Vocation Director
Daughters of St. Paul
50 Saint Pauls Avenue
Boston, MA 02130-3491
(617) 522-8911
e-mail: vocations@pauline.org
or visit www.pauline.org

Pauline
BOOKS & MEDIA

The Daughters of St. Paul operate book and media centers at the following addresses. Visit, call or write the one nearest you today, or find us on the World Wide Web, www.pauline.org

CALIFORNIA
3908 Sepulveda Blvd, Culver City, CA 90230   310-397-8676
5945 Balboa Avenue, San Diego, CA 92111   858-565-9181
46 Geary Street, San Francisco, CA 94108   415-781-5180

FLORIDA
145 S.W. 107th Avenue, Miami, FL 33174   305-559-6715

HAWAII
1143 Bishop Street, Honolulu, HI 96813   808-521-2731
Neighbor Islands call: 800-259-8463

ILLINOIS
172 North Michigan Avenue, Chicago, IL 60601   312-346-4228

LOUISIANA
4403 Veterans Blvd, Metairie, LA 70006   504-887-7631

MASSACHUSETTS
Rte. 1, 885 Providence Hwy, Dedham, MA 02026   781-326-5385

MISSOURI
9804 Watson Road, St. Louis, MO 63126   314-965-3512

NEW JERSEY
561 U.S. Route 1, Wick Plaza, Edison, NJ 08817   732-572-1200

NEW YORK
150 East 52nd Street, New York, NY 10022   212-754-1110
78 Fort Place, Staten Island, NY 10301   718-447-5071

OHIO
2105 Ontario Street, Cleveland, OH 44115   216-621-9427

PENNSYLVANIA
9171-A Roosevelt Blvd, Philadelphia, PA 19114   215-676-9494

SOUTH CAROLINA
243 King Street, Charleston, SC 29401   843-577-0175

TENNESSEE
4811 Poplar Avenue, Memphis, TN 38117   901-761-2987

TEXAS
114 Main Plaza, San Antonio, TX 78205   210-224-8101

VIRGINIA
1025 King Street, Alexandria, VA 22314   703-549-3806

CANADA
3022 Dufferin Street, Toronto, Ontario, Canada M6B 3T5   416-781-9131
1155 Yonge Street, Toronto, Ontario, Canada M4T 1W2   416-934-3440

¡También somos su fuente para libros, videos y música en español!